DUCATI

OSPREY

ALAN CATHCART
Foreword by Franco Farnè

DUCATI

THE UNTOLD STORY
Factory Racers, Prototypes and Specials

Published in 1987 by Osprey Publishing Limited
27A Floral Street, London WC2E 9DP
Member company of the George Philip Group

British Library Cataloguing in Publication Data

Cathcart, Alan
    Ducati: the untold story.
    1. Ducati motorcycle—History
    I. Title
    629.2'275   TL448.D8
ISBN 0-85045-789-0

Editor Tony Thacker
Design David Tarbutt

Filmset by Tameside Filmsetting Limited,
Ashton-under-Lyne, Lancashire
Printed in Hong Kong

Page 1
Mario's Restaurant stands beside Lake Varese, next to the
Cagiva factory for which it acts as a sort of extension to the
works canteen, as well as a dormitory for guests and visiting
journalists. The *spaghetti ai frutti dei laghi* has to be tasted to be
believed

Pages 2–3
The 1980 Montjuich winner gave a superb ride, like a
superfast 900 road bike

Right
World-class Grand Prix and endurance racer, development
engineer and team manager, Franco Farnè was for more than a
quarter of a century Ing. Taglioni's right-hand man at
Meccanica Ducati. Now Dr T's youthful successor Massimo
Bordi can draw on Farnè's unparalleled experience in
producing the next generation of Ducati motorcycles

Foreword

For 30 years, Ducati motorcycles have been my life, first working under Ing. Fabio Taglioni, then more recently with his successor Ing. Massimo Bordi.

During this time I have been a part of the fantastic development of the Ducati marque, then witnessed its decline in the face of the Japanese attack on world markets during the 1970s, and finally the problems brought about by the constant changes of management and control.

Today, thanks to the enthusiasm of the brothers Claudio and Gianfranco Castiglioni, Ducati is entering a new era, with its future assured as the flagship of 'La Moto Italiana'.

I am truly delighted to be part of this revival in the company's fortunes.

It gives me pleasure to contribute this foreword to the second book about Ducati by my friend Alan Cathcart, inasmuch as it records, mainly in photographic form, the work that we in the Reparto Sperimentale have contributed over the years, in an effort to maintain Ducati's reputation for sound and imaginative engineering, as well as catalogues the attachment to the marque on the part of *ducatisti* all over the world.

Fortunately, this is a book about a living, existing marque, not one on those many others which have been lost forever in recent years as a result of such extreme competition from the Orient.

I am proud to have played a role in the Ducati story—both known and unknown—and hope that our efforts will bring continued success in the future.

Ducati motorcycles have a glorious past, as this book shows, but far more important for all of us at Borgo Panigale is the glorious future that we hope so much to attain.

Franco Farnè
Bologna, 1 June 1987

Acknowledgements

Putting together a book like this would not have been possible without the help of the various people at Meccanica Ducati who have made my many visits to Borgo Panigale over the years so fruitful—and exciting. So, sincere thanks for all their much appreciated co-operation and hospitality to Ing. Fabio Taglioni, Franco Farnè (who also did me the honour of writing the foreword to this book), Franco Valentini, Ing. Massimo Bordi, the lovely and gracious Nadia Pavignani, and my chum Giuliano Pedretti. This book is a testament to their dedication to the Ducati name and the engineering excellence it stands for. Thanks too must go to the men who rescued Ducati from its financial abyss and assured the existence of the marque, Gianfranco and Claudio Castiglioni, who carry the hopes of so many enthusiasts around the world for the future of 'La Moto Italiana': their generosity in allowing me to ride and write about so many exciting Ducati and Cagiva prototypes is greatly appreciated.

The assistance of several *ducatisti* outside Italy has also been invaluable, not only in compiling this book, but also in terms of furthering my own enthusiasm for riding, racing and writing about Ducatis. Top of the list must be the Tunstall family, Syd, Ivy and Malcolme, who allowed me to race 'Old Yellow' in American BoTT events for so many years, and on limited resources have carved a name for themselves in the Ducati Hall of Fame. Their great rivals Reno Leoni and Jimmy Adamo have also helped me on many occasions in the past, and I thank them as well as the doyen of British *ducatisti*, Steve Wynne, whose foresight and close touch with the people who actually buy and ride Ducatis on the street has often enabled him to come up with new models when the factory hesitated and declined to take the risk.

Finally, I am grateful for their help to the people who, besides my own photos which appear in this book together with those of the photographers who have collaborated with me on Ducati test stories—Emilio Jimenez, Kel Edge and Phil Masters—kindly sent me their own pictures or allowed me to rummage through their files to find an elusive print. So thanks also to Rolf im Brahm, producer of the beautiful Ducati calendar each year; Claudio Boet and Javier Herrero of *Motociclismo*; Paul Dean of *Cycle World*; Katsuji Ono of *Clubman*, and the many other *ducatisti* around the world who have written to me over the years.

Left

The author hard at work on the Bimota DB1 factory racer at Misano. The handling was effortless, permitting the rider to take the bike to the limit of his own abilities

Below

Starting a second decade racing Ducati V-twins, the author rounds Turn 6 at the Daytona Speedway en route to fifth place in the 1986 Battle of the Twins race on 'Old Yellow', Syd Tunstall's 883 cc valve-spring Sport which, in more than a decade of competition, has never failed to finish a race

Introduction

Few of the world's motorcycle marques, either present or past, have excited such interest and passion in so many countries as Ducati. Far out of proportion to the Borgo Panigale factory's recent production figures, Ducati motorcycles have a worldwide following on the part of motorcycling *cognoscenti* who appreciate good engineering, technical innovation and exciting styling.

Above
The author about to cross the threshold of Meccanica Ducati's holy of holies: the 'Reparto Sperimentale', Borgo Panigale's Experimental Department which also serves as R & D headquarters and factory race shop, all combined in one

Left
'Dr T'—engineer, designer, wine connoisseur and horticulturalist, as well as the world's leading exponent of desmodromic valve design: Ing. Fabio Taglioni, the father of Ducati motorcycles

My first book, *Ducati Motorcycles* (also published by Osprey), explored for the first time in print the full history of the marque from its inception during World War 2, up to the time of the Cagiva takeover. In this second volume, the words play a supporting role to the pictures, most of them never previously published, which further document the untold story of Ducati motorcycles. Factory prototypes never put into production, works racers which have escaped into private hands, others pictured during their active racing career, ingenious and often remarkably professional specials wrought by privateers on the basic Ducati theme, future road models seen at the time of their pre-production track tests or press launch—all these are shown in photos printed here which I have collected over a 20-year period of hopeless addiction to the Bologna cause. I only hope that they are as fascinating for you, the reader, to see here in print as they have been for me to track down and obtain, and that those who might not otherwise fully recognize the prolific talents of Dr T and the home Ducati engineer alike, will see this book as a testament to their efforts.

Alan Cathcart
London, April 1987

Five generations of Ducati emblems

Left
'The accessibility of the Ducati engine on the rare occasions that any mechanical work is required, is incomparable.' Quote from a 1971 Ducati V-twin press handout!

A great moment in Ducati sporting history: Marco Lucchinelli on the Misano rostrum, close to tears after scoring a last-ditch victory against the might of Japan Inc. in the first round of the 1986 TT F1 World Championship. Below, Cagiva boss Gianfranco Castiglioni looks very satisfied at his team's win

Another good reason for journalists to write about Ducati— 'La Nadia': PR high priestess Nadia Pavignani, who for some inexplicable reason is also remarkably camera-shy!

Right

Taglioni's first Ducati, the 98 cc ohc 'Marianna', more formally known as the 100 Gran Sport. Owned by Italian collector Pino Moretti, this remarkably original example of the 1955 model introduced an engine format and crankcase design that was the basis of all Ducati singles for two decades

Below

The Marianna proved devastatingly successful in Italian long-distance races like the Milano–Taranto and Giro d'Italia, prepared as shown here with full lighting equipment for night sections. The 1280 mm wheelbase made for quick handling, especially on the 17 in. wheels which predated today's fashion, while the 18-litre steel fuel tank gave a range of 670 km between stops. With a 20 mm Dell'Orto carb and 8.5:1 compression ratio, output of the little 49.4 × 52 mm engine was 8 bhp at the rear wheel, at 9000 rpm. Within a year of its début, the Marianna became literally unbeatable in its class in Italian production racing, leading in due course to the first desmos

Previous page

A unique matched pair of Ducati desmo 125 factory racers, belonging to Guernsey enthusiast Maurice Ogier. On the left is his 1957 desmo single, on the right the later twin

Below

Taglioni first experimented with desmodromics, or positively-actuated valve gear, while still at the rival Mondial company in 1954. After moving to Ducati, he continued his development of the concept, after first producing a dohc 125 cc valve-spring version of the Marianna engine, the Grand Prix Bialbero, bored out to 55.3 mm. A desmodromic version of this engine was introduced in 1956, winning its début race in the Swedish GP in the hands of Gianni degli Antoni before contesting the 1957–58 world 125 cc title, which it narrowly failed to win. This is a 1957 machine, identified by the frame's single front downtube, bifurcating into a twin-loop cradle

Right

The nature of the triple-camshaft design is clearly evident here. As on all Ducati ohc singles, camshaft drive is by vertical

shaft and bevel gears on the other (right) side of the engine. However, instead of the more compact single-cam/four-lobe layout used on later desmos, on the 125s Taglioni employed three camshafts with the opening cams mounted on the two outer shafts, and both closing lobes on the single central one. The result was the elimination of valve bounce, enabling riders of the little 125 desmos to rev them as high as 15,000 rpm on the overrun without the valves tangling. Ultimately, the desmo single yielded 18 bhp at 12,500 rpm

Overleaf

The tiny 1220 mm wheelbase of Maurice Ogier's 125 desmo makes it hard for any but a midget-sized rider to tuck himself away comfortably on it! Weighing only 81 kg dry, the bike can be pulled up very smartly with the combined aid of the desmo valve gear (allowing full engine braking to be used with impunity) and the 180 mm 2LS Amadoro front brake. The bike pulls well from 8000 rpm upwards; with a five-speed gearbox fitted to this machine (later ones had a six-speeder), performance was remarkable for a mid-1950s ultra-lightweight

Above

Maurice Ogier's desmo 125 twin, one of only three such factory machines built, is the bike raced by Franco Villa into third place on its début in the 1958 Italian GP, a race dominated by Ducatis which filled the first five places. Thereafter it was purchased by Stan Hailwood for son Mike to race, but he preferred the desmo single as being easier to ride. Syd Lawton bought it in turn for *his* son Barry to cut his racing teeth on, before passing it on to Dennis Trollope who rode it in the TT and other races in the late 1960s. After this, it ended up in the USA, before the author found it and brought it back to the UK in 1978. After total restoration, Maurice Ogier acquired it in a trade in 1982, and races it today

Far right

Two of everything does not necessarily mean twice the power: best output for the 125 desmo twin was just 22.5 bhp at 14,000 rpm, with a much narrower powerband than the single, at the expense of increased weight (98 kg dry) and complication. Camshaft drive is by a train of gears between the cylinders, though the triple-cam layout is maintained. The built-up roller-bearing crankshaft uses Hirth couplings, a strong but high-precision design feature also used on the NSU Rennmax twins of the early 1950s. The 42.5 × 45 mm unit breathes through twin 23 mm Dell'Orto carbs (compared

to the single 27 mm unit on the one-cylinder bike), with specially-made flat-sided remote floats to keep overall width to a minimum

Below

An oil-bath clutch lurks behind this handsomely-inscribed outer cover on the 125 desmo twin with six-speed gearbox

Previous page
At 1270 mm, the 125 desmo twin's wheelbase is scarcely rangy, but a little more comfortable for the taller rider than the single's. Top speed of 112 mph was considerably greater than the single's 107 mph, but could only be obtained with a long run-up on a fast track. Overall, the single was much the better bike, if not quite so meaty-looking

Left
The 125 desmo twin was itself derived from an earlier 175 cc valve-spring design built for the 1957 Giro d'Italia, in which it was unsuccessfully ridden by Leopoldo Tartarini, today the boss of the Italjet concern. Two machines were built, one of which found its way to the USA where it lives today, the other remaining in the factory until it was acquired by the Villa brothers, Franco and Walter, who converted it to a 250 for the 1964 season. Before they had a chance to race it, they secured a contract with Mondial to race a factory-backed team for them instead, leaving the Ducati twin sidelined.

Somehow it found its way to South Africa, whence the author rescued it in 1985. This photo was taken before the current restoration task was commenced. Note the dohc layout and dry clutch

Above
Equally rare was the Spanish-built four-cylinder 250 cc racer, constructed by Ducati's Mototrans subsidiary and known as the MT 250. Rider Bruno Spaggiari made a desultory appearance in practice for the 1967 Spanish GP at Barcelona's Montjuich Park aboard the bike, but opted to race his desmo single instead. After a year of further development, the 44.5 × 40 mm machine, which produced a claimed 50 bhp at 14,000 rpm, appeared once again at Montjuich for the 1968 Spanish classic: here is a rare shot of Spaggiari in action on it once again before it was withdrawn after a few practice laps. Its present whereabouts are unknown: can any Iberian *ducatista* solve the mystery?

Previous page

One of the many Ducati prototypes over the years which got built, then aborted, was the massive 1257 cc V4 pushrod ohv Apollo, designed by Taglioni in 1962 at the behest of the company's US distributors, the Berliner Corporation. The idea was to produce a bike which, like the V7 Moto Guzzi a decade later, could be sold to US police departments as well as in civilian form as a highway cruiser. Though boasting several avant-garde features, when launched in 1964 the result was an unhappy marriage of Italian engineering and transatlantic styling. Even so, the engine's performance (80 bhp at 6000 rpm in basic trim with a single 24 mm carb for each pair of cylinders front and rear; over 100 bhp in four-carb 'Sport' form) would have been sufficient to gain it widespread commercial approval, but for the inability of the massive 5.00 × 16 in. Pirelli whitewall tyres to transmit the horsepower to the road without throwing a tread. This factory photo of the single prototype made shows the original ritzy gold paint job in all its glory, as well as the relatively compact 1530 mm wheelbase

Left

A year later, in 1965, the Apollo had been redesigned around a less powerful (65 bhp) engine, though the four-carb Sport unit is fitted in this photo taken in the Berliner's New Jersey warehouse. The reduced output meant that it no longer had a performance advantage over the lighter, smaller and less powerful British twins, ruling out its civilian use, even if the revised Pirelli tyres seemed to have cured their tread-throwing tendency. The model would still have been entirely viable for police use in the USA and Canada though, but it was scrapped in 1965 as the result of political infighting in Italy

Above right

Franco Valentini has been Export Sales Manager for Meccanica Ducati for two decades, a position he still holds today under the new Cagiva management. More to the point, he has devoted his life to the marque, having been a Ducati dealer in the early 1950s before going to work for the factory. It was he who recognized the importance of the factory prototypes shown in the following pages and prevented them being thrown out for scrap in early 1984. 'I looked out of an upstairs window and saw a truck outside being loaded with what looked like a lot of junk,' relates Franco. 'But I could see already in the truck what looked like a prototype four-cylinder engine, with another just about to be thrown in. I was horrified at this possible destruction of Ducati heritage, so I ran down the stairs, three at a time, through the factory, and was just able to stop the men driving away to the scrap-yard. Now I hope one day we can establish a Ducati museum somewhere in or near the factory where these artifacts can be displayed.' On behalf of all *ducatisti* everywhere, Franco— *tantissime grazie!*

After the cancellation of the Apollo project, and the equally abortive 125 cc four-cylinder racer, Taglioni stayed away from more than two cylinders until 1976, when he designed this single-ohc, parallel-valve, 90-degree desmo V4, with water-cooling via a pump located in front of the engine, and Pantah-type belt drive to the camshafts. Designed to be built in either 750 cc or 1000 cc form, this part-metal, part-wood mock-up got as far as being placed in a single-tube open-cradle frame, using the engine as a fully-stressed member

The water-cooled V4 had one Dell'Orto 40 mm carb per bank of cylinders. However, company management felt that water-cooling was too cumbersome and bulky, even though Taglioni argued in favour of it as helping to meet future noise regulations. Ten years on, it is *de rigueur* on Japanese performance bikes, and Ducati's own next-generation V-twin features liquid-cooling!

Instead, Taglioni turned to a partially oil-cooled design, later imitated by Suzuki on their GSX-R, designed and developed from 1978 onwards. In four-carburettor 1000 cc form, this gave no less than 131 bhp at 12,000 rpm on the testbed, again as a belt-driven sohc desmo. This shows the stage which chassis development reached in 1981 before the project was finally scrapped on the grounds of cost and doubts over the continued existence of Ducati motorcycles, prior to the Cagiva takeover

V4 chassis design was a sturdy, fully-triangulated spaceframe, closely based on the 600TT2 racer; note the monoshock rear suspension. Taglioni also built a 500 cc parallel twin-cylinder version, using the two rear cylinders on a new crankcase. This yielded 73 bhp, again at the rear wheel, but appears to have been thrown out after being discontinued. His intention was to fuel-inject the V4 unit, using a specially-built SPICA pump, and 150 bhp would surely have been on tap. Ironically, a governing factor in the decision to scrap the V4 was the early-1970s swing by Japanese manufacturers towards the 750 cc class: it was felt that the oil-cooled V4 Ducati would be too big and heavy to scale down successfully, but now of course the main emphasis today is on 1-litre performance megabikes like the GPZ1000RX, CBR1000, FZR1000 and GSX-R1100. A 150 bhp 1000 cc V4 Ducati would have found a worthy market

Two views of the oil-cooled V4 prototype, one example of which still sits in the Reparto Sperimentale on a stand, just as it was last bench-tested. This design used a single plain-bearing crankshaft, with massive dry multiplate clutch

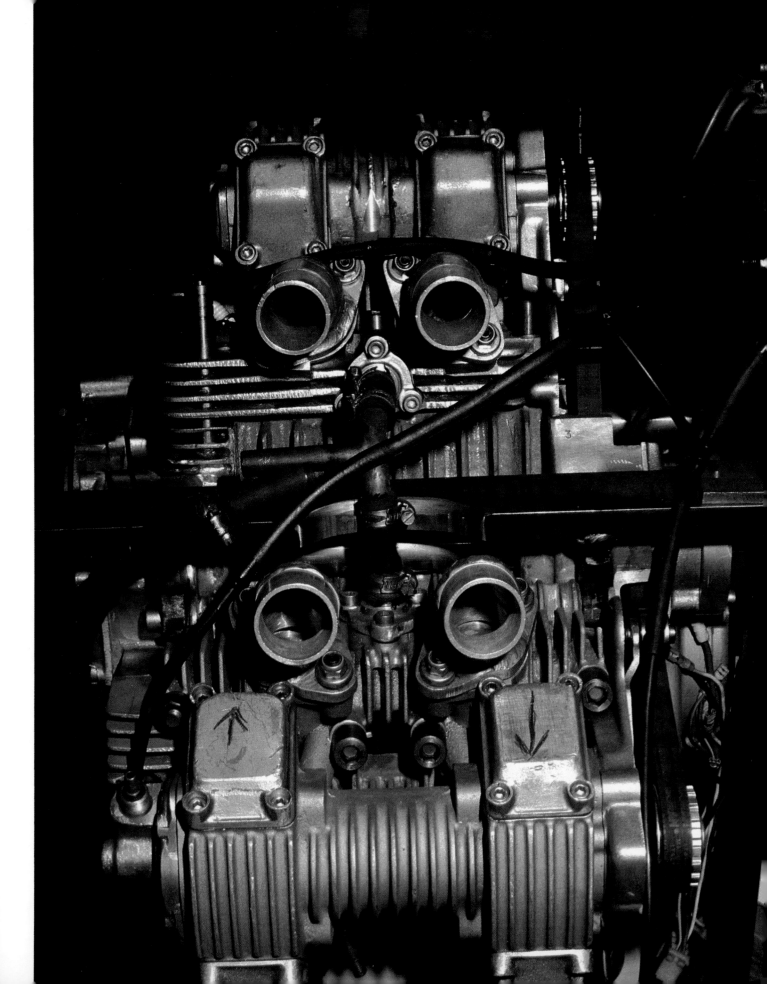

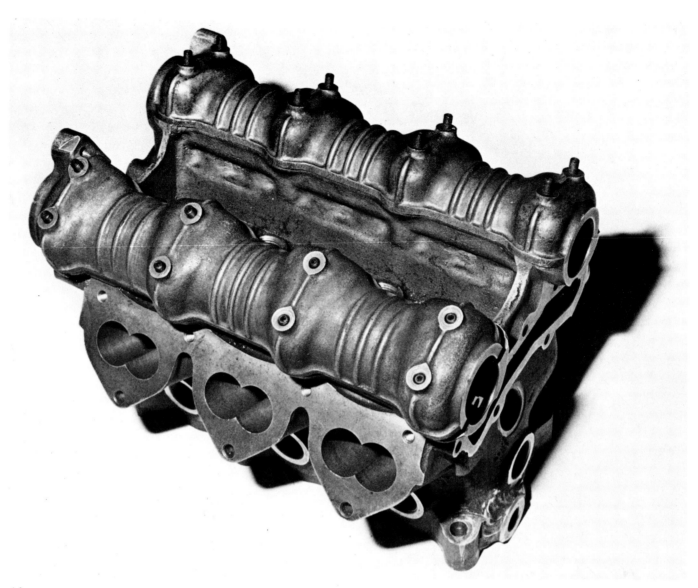

Above

The one and only three-cylinder Ducati was an abortive 350 cc GP racing prototype based on an engine design bought in from the British Ricardo engineering design company in 1971 by the Managing Director of Ducati at that time, the race-mad Fredmano Spairani. Taglioni voiced objections to the design from the outset, especially when it was discovered that Ricardo's 12-valve, water-cooled, dohc prototype unit would barely deliver 30 bhp, and not the 50 bhp promised for it nor the 50–55 bhp of a good TD3 Yamaha, which also had the advantage of being much lighter.

It would also not run properly with fuel injection, which Taglioni felt was the only way for a four-stroke to remain on competitive terms with the two-stroke opposition. After two years' development, the best that could be extracted from the design was just over 50 bhp at 14,500 rpm—insufficient for the resultantly heavy bike to be competitive. The idea of a new generation of Ducati triples for the road, based on a successful GP machine, was therefore quietly dropped—though not before development of the Pantah had been set back a year or so as a result

Right

This solitary cylinder head, recently used as a doorstop in the Ducati design department, is all that appears to remain of the abortive Ricardo-inspired 350 triple

Above

Ducati never had much luck with parallel twins, whether in road or race form. This is their first unsuccessful attempt to provide the Berliner Corporation and their American customers with an Italianate Triumph or Latin Norton, then perceived as being the approved route to commercial success in the mid-1960s US market. Displayed at Daytona in March 1965, this 500 cc twin was also intended for production in 750 cc form, which might explain the massive crankcases (with hefty oil sump beneath) and, surprisingly, just a four-speed gearbox. The pushrod ohv unit was massively over-engineered, yielded only 36 bhp at 6500 rpm, and in 360-degree form, as shown here, vibrated considerably. A 180-degree version, intended to produce more power, shook even more!

Electric starting was used for the first time by Ducati on the 1965 prototype 500, the starter motor slotting into the gap in front of the crankcases as seen here. This lengthened the wheelbase of the complete bike unreasonably, which together with the engine's width and the low-slung exhaust pipes, severely inhibited cornering. A disaster! The engine number of this sole prototype can just be discerned on the upper left crankcase: DM500USA!

Below

Ducati's second go at a parallel twin, this time with Taglioni in full charge of the project, was their best ever. Sadly, by late 1968 when this Mk 2 version appeared, the rules of the game had changed and the bike never really had a chance. Still, as pushrod ohv 500 cc twins go, this was quite a decent bike, being lighter, smaller and more powerful than its ungainly, inept predecessor. Instead of the 1965 version's 72 × 58.8 mm dimensions, this later machine used standard 250 cc Ducati cylinder sizes of 74 × 57.8 mm, yielded 38 bhp at 6500 rpm, yet weighed 18 kg less and had a top

speed of 103 mph. It also handled properly, but by then the market for such a bike was, probably correctly, perceived as having disappeared with the arrival of the CB450 Honda and suchlike on the scene

Below

The decision to discontinue the Ducati single-cylinder range in the mid-1970s seems especially short-sighted today, when such machines powered by Japanese, Austrian and even, yes, Italian engines are so much in vogue for both on- and off-road use. Taglioni fought bitterly, but unsuccessfully, against this decision, having already designed the unit shown here, a 500 cc single-cam desmo with bevel drive to the camshaft and what is essentially a rear cylinder from a 900 V-twin (but with full finning) mounted on a specially-made crankcase with five-speed gearbox

Below right

These bulky sidecovers of the mid-1970s 500 desmo would have been slimmed down for production. The prototype yielded 52 bhp at the rear wheel, at 9000 rpm

Left

An alternative to the belt-driven ohc Pantah line would have been this 1976 860 cc V-twin, with chain drive to the single overhead camshafts. As can be clearly seen, the design was a valve-spring rather than desmodromic one, intended to create a new line of V-twin Ducatis that would be less expensive to manufacture than the costly bevel-drive desmos and, without the supposed complication of desmo valve gear, would appeal to a wider market. The project was dropped after Taglioni successfully argued that a non-desmo Ducati would alienate more customers than it attracted

Below

The idea of building a modern single-cylinder bike in both trail and roadster form by using the rear cylinder off a V-twin was always one of Taglioni's pet projects, and it almost reached fruition. This is the early 1970s prototype for the Utah street enduro model which was launched at the 1977

Milan Show but scrapped shortly afterwards. The 83 × 64 mm 346 cc engine effectively comprises the rear cylinder of the Pantah prototype V-twin, with belt-driven sohc desmo cylinder head, mounted in a modified Street Scrambler frame with cast-alloy wheels and drum brakes. This engine yielded 27 bhp at 8500 rpm but was obviously capable of more

Overleaf

In its final form, as displayed at Milan in 1977, the Utah was the forerunner of today's boulevard enduros; with its accent on street rather than trail use, it had small-diameter disc brakes and full lighting equipment. Curiously for such a good-looking bike, its aesthetics were what ultimately told against it. According to Dr T, factory management did not like the way the cambelt cover 'pointed backwards'—obviously a *good* reason to scrap this accomplished prototype. Wouldn't a bike like this sell in viable numbers for Ducati today?

Above

The Utah was displayed at Milan in company with its cousin, the Rollah, a roadster version of the same design. This seems to have been scrapped or, more likely, to have 'escaped' from the factory after being aborted, because there is no sign of it today at Borgo Panigale

Right

Ducati were often criticized by some people in Italy for concentrating too much on performance lightweights in the late 1950s and early 1960s, when others, even MV Agusta, offered a more humble 'cooking' motorcycle. Ducati kept the ageing pushrod 100 on the books well into the 1960s, but in reality they were only using up existing stocks. Here is what remains of its projected successor, a pushrod 125 cc engine designed by Taglioni in 1958 or 1959 (he's not sure!), with typical early-Ducati bottom end and a four-speed gearbox. 'It was rather noisy, but a very good engine,' judges Dr T. In the end, though, it was decided to offer an exclusively ohc motorcycle range, and the ohv prototype was scrapped

Above

Persistent rumours down the years have repeatedly tantalized enthusiasts with promises of a shaft-drive, touring, Pantah-based model. If, or now more likely when, it finally comes, chances are it will be closely based on this 650 police model, with full fairing and panniers, offered to the *carabinieri* of the world in 1985. It still had chain drive, though

Left

This 200 cc industrial engine dates from the late 1950s, and according to Ing. Taglioni, it is one of the more-than-1000 different engines he has designed down the years since his first in 1948 of which he is the most proud. 'It was a fantastic unit, which gave good power but at the expense of very low fuel consumption,' he recalls. 'But then the decision was made to pursue a diesel-engine development programme, and we did not persevere with it. A pity.'

47

Top left

The British Heron Suzuki 500 is often accredited with being the first motorcycle to be built with a chassis constructed from CIBA-Geigy M-Board aluminium honeycomb, but others were there before, including Ducati. This is the unique chassis designed and built by Italian frame specialist Luigi Segale in 1980, at the request of Ducati management, to accommodate the 600TT2 racing version of the Pantah engine for TT Formula racing. The sheets of M-Board are riveted together with alloy strips, and a magnesium swing arm is fitted which pivots on the chassis rather than on the engine cases, as on the production Pantah; Segale's favoured Fox Shocks are fitted, two-up, at the rear, with Marzocchi front forks and a honeycomb fork brace! The design is a full monocoque, with the 20 litres of fuel permitted by TT2 regulations carried in the forward section of the chassis. Sadly, this avant-garde prototype was never given a fair chance to prove itself, Taglioni claiming that the nature of the design caused overheating of the rear cylinder: in view of the DB1 Bimota and Ducati's own experience with the all-enveloped Paso, this seems unsubstantiated. More likely, some professional jealousy resulted in the Segale prototype being dropped in favour of the Verlicchi-built spaceframe eventually adopted, which was designed in-house

Bottom left

If the Berliner brothers had still been in charge of Ducati's North American sales in the early 1980s when the custom bike craze hit the USA, maybe they would have persuaded the Ducati management to produce something like this—or there again, maybe not! Give the French chopper freak who built this, er, ultra-long wheelbase special a hand for quality of execution, though. The engine is a 450 valve-springer

Above

In due course, Ducati did get around to building a street custom, largely at the behest of Gianfranco Castiglioni, a fan of this kind of machine. In fact, the solitary DB900 prototype, shown here in the yard of the Cagiva factory, was built on commission in the USA by a well-known custom shop, then shipped to Italy. The engine is a bevel-drive 860 from the Mike Hailwood Replica, a later version of which (with the 973 cc Mille engine) stands behind. The decision to discontinue production of this bevel-drive ohc desmo power unit, expensive to manufacture in the 1980s, led to the DB900 project being dropped not long after it was finished in 1985

Above

Instead, Ducati produced the Indiana, using the 650 cc version of the Pantah engine (also available as a 350 for Japan and the home market). The deft hand of Massimo Tamburini, the former Bimota designer who moved to Cagiva in 1985, made a good-looking bike out of the acres of chrome. . .

Left

. . . and one that went, stopped and handled better than any other middleweight custom on the market apart from the Suzuki Intruder. Once a hardened *ducatista* overcame his prejudice against a neo-American desmo long enough to actually ride it, chances were he'd be hooked. As a bike for boulevards or a gentle meander in the country, it had few equals

As has so often been the case, a Ducati owner actually showed the factory what they might have done: this fully-faired, French-registered 900 is a serious touring machine by any standards. Cast wheels might have been an advantage with all that extra weight, but apart from that, and the chain drive, it is hard to fault

On the other hand . . . well, at least it's different! A French
enthusiast's tricked-out swinging single, a 250 special with
cantilever monoshock rear end, box-section tubular chassis,
cast wheels and high-rise pipe. It went OK at this Croix-en-
Ternois meeting in June 1986, too

Below
Light years away in execution, if not in concept, is American Roger Sears' 600 Pantah, seen here in 1983 in the Daytona infield. The following year Roger converted the bike to racing specification. Using the same Canadian-built Wolf frame for US Battle of the Twins racing, he won the Lightweight BoTT race at Daytona in 1985 by a huge margin, as well as the US national title in his class. Thereupon he retired from racing and converted the bike back to street trim—only even prettier than before

Above

For several years, the factory's reluctance to capitalize on the success of their alluring 600TT2 racer in TT2 competition all over the world was one of the more inexplicable aspects of Ducati's seemingly non-existent marketing philosophy. Inevitably, someone else came up with the first TT2 for the road. Opinions are divided as to just who that someone was, but long-time Ducati guru Steve Wynne (seen talking to rider Steve Tonkin on the left) was certainly in the vanguard with this Harris-framed street replica of the factory race bike, whose frame geometry was exactly duplicated with a couple of minor strengthening tubes. The engine was a standard 600 cc Pantah, but the specification of engine and cycle parts was capable of almost infinite variation

Left

Wynne's company, Sports Racing Motorcycles, painted the prototype in Cagiva colours on its launch in early 1984 to try to attract some interest and help from the new owners of Ducati. It sort of worked, but most owners preferred the more traditional red and yellow livery. The later bikes had 750 cc engines as well

The success of the Sports Ducati (Cagiva?) and other low-volume street replicas of the 'Verlicchi'-framed TT2 persuaded the Castiglionis to consider the feasibility of producing their own sports bike, but in updated form and designed more specifically for street use than a barely sanitized racer with lights. Instead of doing it in-house, though, they commissioned a design around the 650 Pantah engine from none other than Bimota, who were going through a hard time financially in 1984 and were hungry for this sort of work. At the same time, Bimota had suffered an internal upheaval, leading to the departure of one of the Rimini firm's founders, designer Massimo Tamburini. The creation of a Bimota-Ducati for Cagiva was thus the first task tackled by his successor, Federico Martini, and this is the result, never before seen publicly

Martini's Bimota project bike unquestionably established the
trend for future desmo V-twin designs; 16 in. wheels, rising-
rate monoshock rear suspension, the latest Marzocchi front
forks and new-generation Brembo brakes, set off by radial
tyres, all combined to produce a machine whose specification
was as dramatic as its looks

The first elements of the distinctive Martini school of motorcycle design, fully expressed in Bimota's own DB1 and later copied by others in the all-enclosed Ducati Paso, Honda Hurricane and the like, are clearly evident here. Note the way the fuel tank blends into the upper fairing: all it takes are some side panels to complete full enclosure of the engine, and the theme is complete. Would Ducati have been better off building this bike as is, rather than evolving it into the Paso? Ironically, by the time the Bimota-Ducati 650 was complete in early 1985, the person who took over its development (or not, as the case might be) was none other than Massimo Tamburini, who by now had joined Cagiva as their head of design development. Human nature perhaps being what it is, it was dropped in favour of the Paso

Above

Meanwhile, the last new Ducati road model to have been produced before the Cagiva takeover was the long-awaited 750 F1 Replica—only, it wasn't. Instead of producing a street version of Tony Rutter's crushingly successful TT2 world champion, a latter-day equivalent of the legendary 750SS, the factory opted instead for a completely new chassis only loosely based on the racing frame. Here is the prototype under construction in the Reparto Sperimentale in the winter of 1984–85; note the swing-arm-mounted passenger footrests—the bike was originally conceived as a two-seater, before common sense prevailed

Right

Resplendent in *tricolore* paintwork, the 750 F1 Replica stands mirrored in Lake Varese soon after the Cagiva takeover was consummated in the spring of 1985. The bold Cagiva lettering was, fortunately, just a thought which was later dropped in favour of accentuating Ducati's own heritage and brand identity

Above

Compare this final production Replica with the prototype on page 60 to see the changes wrought by development. This bike was never a best-seller, though—the DB1 Bimota stole the limelight. Cantilever rear suspension was a disappointment, and by then outmoded

Right

Wouldn't you really have a Bimota? Well, er, yes—if you could afford the not-inconsiderable price tag. Arguably the best-looking Ducati-engined motorcycle ever built, the DB1 also completely changed the fortunes of the small Rimini company, taking them from bankruptcy to financial stability in two short years. What's more, the handling was so good you never had to worry about running out of road. . .

Previous page

Like soldiers about to be drilled, here is a good chunk of the total 750 F1 Replica production on parade at Borgo Panigale, about to be clothed with their bodywork and crated. Those are 650 Pantah seats in the background

Left

Bimota boss Giuseppe Morri (left) and designer Federico Martini pose with the road and race versions of the DB1 at the testing début of the street version at Misano in August 1985. No wonder Martini looks pleased: the bike went on to set new bench-marks in terms of Ducati handling and performance

Below left

The TT F1 version of the Bimota DB1 has an alloy sub-section for the seat, GPM-designed dry clutch, Marzocchi M1R suspension, 42.5 mm Dell'Ortos and reworked cylinder heads with Ducati factory race cams. Riders Tardozzi and Matteoni inflicted some morale-boosting defeats on the works Ducatis in hard-fought Italian TT1 races, but were less successful abroad

Below

Spot the differences. The DB1 in street trim had the same basic layout and geometry as the racer from which it was developed—only the hardware was changed

Designed by Massimo Tamburini, the Paso utilized an unlovely square-section steel tube frame, fully enclosed with slightly bulbous bodywork. The carburettor was a twin-choke Weber specially developed for the V-twin engine. The Paso set new standards of comfort, ride and civilized appeal for a Ducati, at less cost than the DB1 and without its uncompromisingly sporting posture

Below

Ducati's riposte to the success of the DB1 was twofold: the Paso for what was hoped to be a mass market, and the Montjuich for the track. Here Franco Farnè gives a final wipe to the 750 Paso, named after former Aermacchi rider Renzo Pasolini, at the bike's press launch in May 1986. The white 350 behind is the factory test hack, while between them is a Montjuich

Overleaf

The ultimate Ducati in the classic mode was surely the Montjuich, though. A hard-nosed but raucously effective street racer with 'the works'. In terms of performance, it really was the long-awaited F1 Replica the factory had promised but failed to deliver. A slightly sanitized version of the works F1 endurance/TT1 racer, it was the 1980s version of the 750SS—at last. But too late?

Compare the so-called F1 Replica with these photos taken in late 1984 of 'the real thing': the factory's 750 F1 racer seen here at Imola in a November test session for Walter Villa and Tony Rutter. Chunky but effective

Above
The new 750 F1 (foreground) compared with its 750TT1 predecessor. The latter had cantilever rear suspension (soon to be replicated on the street bike), the newer machine having the more supple rising-rate system

Overleaf
The old and the new—but both are handsome motorcycles by any standards

Above

A factory 750 F1 engine, fitted with magnesium casting for NCR dry clutch. The clutch basket had a tendency to fracture and required a steel sleeve to be shrunk over it for complete peace of mind. The engine produced 95 bhp at the rear wheel, at 10,000 rpm, yet thanks to the legendary Ducati torque and mile-wide powerband was competitive with 130 bhp-plus Japanese fours on all but the fastest circuits

Right

Ducati factory race mechanic Giuliano Pedretti working on Lucchinelli's 750 F1 Replica mount for the 1986 Daytona 200 Superbike race: he qualified, but retired in the race. Pedretti has been a stalwart of the Ducati race shop for more than 15 years, and his careful preparation of factory racers down the years has played a vital part in Ducati's racing success. He is also a very cheerful bloke, a factor not to be ignored when it's 2 am in the Montjuich 24 Horas and your bike is five laps in the lead. . .

Above

A phalanx of Dukes at Daytona in 1986. Left is Lucchinelli's 851 cc factory bike, in the middle is Jimmy Adamo on a similar machine but with an 818 cc (92 × 61.5 mm) engine, while on the right is Stefano Caracchi (son of Reno, the 'C' in NCR—Nepoti and Caracchi Racing) on the 750 cc Tecfar, with Spanish-built chassis designed by Antonio Cobas (see page 98). Lucky won, Adamo fell off on the banking contesting second place with Paul Lewis' wailing Cosworth, and Caracchi ran low on petrol when challenging for fourth place; he eventually finished fifth

Overleaf

Marco Lucchinelli sweeps round Daytona's Turn 6 en route to victory in the 1986 Battle of the Twins race, aboard his factory F1 racer, fitted with experimental air-cooled 851 cc Pantah engine, measuring 92 × 64 mm rather than the 750's 90 × 61.5 mm. Its output was only slightly up, at 97 bhp, but torque and mid-range were improved

Above

Adamo's sponsor Reno Leoni has kept the Ducati flag flying high in the USA for more than a decade, first in Superbike, then latterly in BoTT racing. One of racing's great characters, with fractured 'spaghetti americano' accent, outsize cigars, wide-brimmed stetsons and on/off moustache, Reno's charisma is matched by his preparation skills. Here he poses happily at Daytona in October 1981 with his 950 cc V-twin desmo, having just secured the first-ever US National BoTT title thanks to the riding talents of Jimmy Adamo. Looks standard, doesn't it? Well, it isn't!

Right

Reno's Big Duke, seen here in 1984 when it briefly became a Cagiva for sponsorship reasons, was ridden by Freddie Spencer, Rich Schlacter, and other notable riders before taking Jimmy Adamo to three US BoTT titles in a row from 1981 to 1983. In the guise shown here, the engine measures 90 × 74.4 mm for a capacity of 947 cc, in which form it yielded 110 bhp at the crank, running at 8500 rpm. A carefully-made chrome-moly frame, exactly duplicating the original, much heavier, steel chassis, permitted weight to be dropped to 320 lb dry—right on the US Superbike limit for 1000 cc twins

Left

Leoni and Adamo pose at Loudoun with their 1985 Superbike, a Cagiva Alazzurra with 750 cc Pantah-based engine which showed remarkable speed by qualifying seventh on the grid for the Daytona 200 that year—but only after the slow factory-built power unit had been traded for one of Reno's specials! The engine sat too far back in the standard Pantah frame for handling to be ideal, but with 95 usable bhp available, this bike was always a threat, especially on slower circuits

Below

The NCR dry clutch (with steel sleeve!) stands out, but note the extra bracing tubes on the chassis, dual ignition and much-needed steering damper on Leoni's Alazzurra. This bike was later sold to privateer Pete Johnson, who won the 1987 Daytona Modified BoTT race with it

Left

For 1986 Reno reverted to his main love, the big twins. Here he is in the Florida twilight firing up his latest baby for the first time. Based on a 973 cc Mille engine with plain-bearing bottom end, the engine is (legally) bored out to 1017 cc for US BoTT races, giving well over 100 bhp at the rear wheel. The special frame has 16 in. wheels and a shorter wheelbase than standard. Adamo led the 1987 Daytona BoTT with this bike before an oil leak sidelined him

Above

Reno Leoni's great rival among transatlantic Ducati tuners is British expatriate Syd Tunstall, whose Derby-born son Malcolme is a fast and determined rider who would have made his mark in GP-class racing had he chosen to try his hand at it instead of following his heart and racing Ducatis. Here, father and son pose with their 1981 BoTT bike, also a 950 featuring many special parts marketed by the Tunstall family via their shop, Syd's Cycles, based in St Petersburg, Florida

Above

Syd Tunstall at Daytona in 1986 with, arguably, one of the most famous Ducati privateer racers in the world: Old Yellow. Originally a humble 1973 valve-spring 750 Sport roadster, the perennially hard-up Tunstalls turned it into a Superbike on which Malcolme won countless races and Florida State titles in the 1970s, as well as placing high up in US National Superbike races and the Daytona 200. In 1979,

the old lady was retired in favour of the newer bike shown in the previous photo, then from 1981 onwards entrusted to the author to race in BoTT events at Daytona and elsewhere, never finishing out of the top six. In over 450 documented races (including heats and finals), Old Yellow has never been dropped nor, even more remarkably, ever failed to finish a race—a fine testament to Syd Tunstall's preparation abilities. Who says Ducatis aren't reliable?

Left

After varying in capacity from 750 to 906 cc, Old Yellow finally became an 883 cc bike, using Imola cams for a desmo (but still a valve-springer) with the closing cams revolving in space. The old warrior, slightly battered but never broken, is still able to give the young 'uns a run for their money and now lives in the UK, where it is eligible for Classic racing

Right

My hero! Syd Tunstall with a flamboyant Dr T at Daytona in 1986, beside the little 350 desmo on which Syd himself won dozens of races throughout the 1970s, winding up with his final Florida State title at the age of 53! The bike is raced just once annually by son Malcolme nowadays, winning a hat trick of Daytona 350 cc Vintage races in 1984–86

Customers still wanted a big twin with a modern chassis and suspension so once again, as with the 750TT1 replica, Steve Wynne stepped in to meet the need by commissioning Harris Engineering to make this Super Imola frame kit, better known as the Monomille. Ceriani front forks and a monoshock rear end with rising-rate White Power suspension, matched to 16 in. wheels and a 57 in. wheelbase, found favour with *ducatisti* all over the world; any bevel-drive engine could be fitted into the frame, permitting you to build your own café racer from the humblest of origins and at reasonable cost

The Manx policeman on point duty at Creg-ny-Baa may not be impressed, but the Monomille was a genuine head-turner everywhere the prototype went in TT Week 1985. The twin-headlight styling was not to everyone's taste, though, and that cut-out in the tank burnt your knee nicely if you tried riding the bike in jeans

Minimalist engineering of the Harris frame is shown clearly here, but the bike was extremely well made, bearing in mind its prototype nature

Above
While US development on the big twins down the years has concentrated on wringing more power and speed from the engine, Europeans have tended to rework the cycle parts in an effort to reduce weight and speed up the handling. Here is an impressive British effort, the 950 cc machine raced by leading British Ducati exponent Dave Railton in UK BoTT events in 1984, built by Eric Dymoke. The DRS chassis has a 16 in. front wheel, monoshock rear end with alloy swing arm, mechanical anti-dive on the front forks and 60 in. wheelbase. Pantah-based machines were more competitive on British short circuits but it was a nice effort

Overleaf
Handling of the Monomille round the Isle of Man TT course was very impressive, so why couldn't the factory have made something like this years before?

Instead, this was to have been their update of the MHR Mille, seen in the Reparto Sperimentale in early 1985. This bike has an 18 in. front wheel fitted for comparison purposes but a 16 in. front was also tried, and it would have been marketed with such until Cagiva stepped in to consummate their purchase later that spring

Whereupon, Cagiva commissioned Massimo Tamburini to produce a Thoroughly Modern Mille, and this is it—or rather, what it would have been, had not the hard-headed decision been taken to discontinue production of the bevel-drive engine on the grounds of cost. Box-section chassis, monoshock rear end, 16 in. wheels, Bimota-esque styling, new-generation Marzocchi suspension, Brembo brakes and Michelin radials, and a 1470 mm wheelbase—it would all have been there, though the design for the exhaust silencer has a question mark over it. Pity

Right

So probable did it appear that the Cagiva Mille would go into production that a preliminary batch of frames were even commissioned. Instead, their overall design layout led directly to the Paso

Aesthetically, this customized Rimini-registered 900 may not be totally successful, but it shows the sort of bike customers were wanting the factory to build. Strictly for runs of less than one kilometre to the nearest café, judging by that exhaust— or maybe he wore asbestos socks?

The 950 cc Tecfar, commissioned by Spanish Ducati guru Ricardo Fargas (right, kneeling), was arguably the ultimate big twin ever built. Designed by Antonio Cobas, this bike was the first bevel-drive Ducati to successfully feature a monoshock rear end, achieved by actually lengthening the already rangy wheelbase to no less than 1560 mm, raising the engine, fitting GP-type rear suspension and steering geometry and 16 in. wheels. The result was a highly competitive motorcycle which brought future 250 cc GP star Carlos Cardus to the forefront of the racing world, enabling him to match and even defeat the best of the four-cylinder Japanese opposition in Spanish Superbike events in 1982: he won the F1 title with six wins from six starts

Delighted with this success, Fargas commissioned another design from Cobas, this time based on the 750TT1 Pantah engine. The result was not initially as successful as the big twin, due to lack of development, but then the Ducati factory acquired it and did the job properly. The result was a superbly-handling bike which took Juan Garriga to pole position and an early lead in the 1985 Montjuich TT1 world round, before becoming involved in the big accident which left Tony Rutter seriously injured. Rebuilt, the 750 Tecfar won the Italian endurance title later that year, then took Stefano Caracchi to fifth in the Daytona BoTT race in 1986, improving to second (in 850 cc form) in the red-flagged race in 1987. Here it is in its original form at the Calafat track in Spain in 1985

Above

Two more attempts at improving on the 750 F1's unsatisfactory cantilever rear end are incorporated in these two quite different racing Pantahs built by Japanese Ducati enthusiast Kas Yajima. Shaded in the January sun at the 1986 BoTT meeting at the tortuous Tsukuba circuit, the two bikes feature variations on the same twin-spar beam frame, made in light alloy with rising-rate monoshock rear end

Overleaf

Even more resourceful, and beautifully executed, were the efforts by Tsuguatsu Mihara, boss of the Tokyo-based Blue Point Racing Team and one of Japan's most loyal Ducati enthusiasts, to improve on the factory's production racing chassis. This is the last of his several efforts in this direction, pictured at the Sugo circuit where it was capable of getting in the top ten of the keenly-contested Japanese TT F1 title rounds in 1986

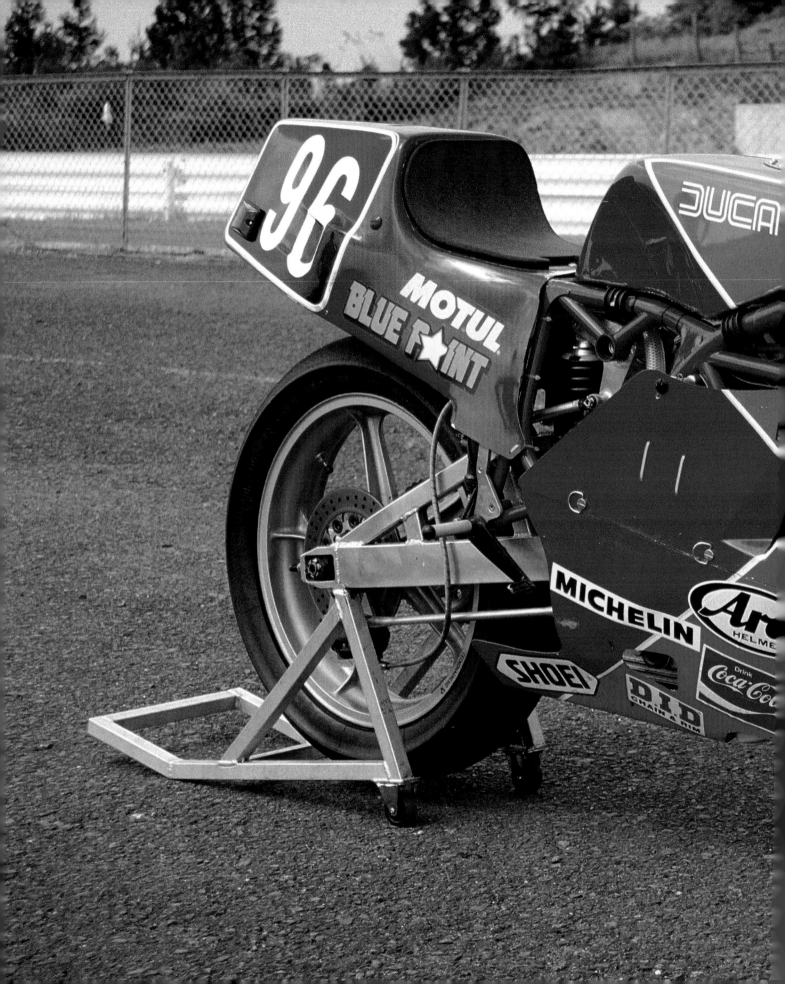

Left

The Blue Point Ducati employs a kitted 750 F1 engine in a chrome-moly chassis, fitted with rising-rate Kayaba rear suspension and the entire front end off an RG500 Suzuki, complete with brake-operated hydraulic anti-dive. A 16 in. front wheel is utilized

Above

Weighing just 138 kg in Suzuka 8-hour endurance trim, complete with lighting equipment and starter, the Blue Point Ducati has Cobas-like forward weight bias of 55/45 per cent and a 25-degree head angle

Right

Attention to detail: the single headlamp on the Blue Point Ducati (only the last hour of the Suzuka race is run in the dark) is rubber-mounted to counter vibration

Even more extreme have been the efforts of Australian Ducati tuner Bob Brown to inflict lasting defeat on the Japanese multis with his succession of desmo V-twins, resulting in the first eight-valve Pantah to be built, in 1985, anywhere in the world. Completely home-brewed by Brown and his friend Darren Andrew-Smith (hence the initials DAS on the cam covers), the four-camshaft, eight-valve, valve-spring heads are fitted to a modified 650 Pantah bottom half, bored and in due course to be stroked to give 750 cc and over. The camshafts use F1 Cosworth DFV profiles, operating valves from a 650 Kawasaki, each using twin S & W valve springs; the cambelts are 8 mm wider than standard, with a new cross-over shaft. The engine is shown here in original form, with a wet clutch and a tubular spaceframe in the process of being wrapped round it

Above

Sure of the success of his project, Brown took a year off from racing in 1985–86 to lick his eight-valve Ducati into shape, commissioning a full monocoque alloy frame from fellow Melbourne resident and former GP mechanic Rod Tingate. This is the result, nearing completion in Tingate's workshop in early 1986, with 20 litres of fuel carried in the twin spars of the beam frame. The engine now has an NCR dry clutch

Overleaf

Bob Brown (dark glasses, centre at rear) is a tuning wizard whose laconic manner disguises a fierce passion for Ducatis. The eight-valve project is by no means the only attempt in his personal campaign against the might of Japan Inc.—sadly, he is not assisted by the Australian Ducati importer or the factory. Why not, *signori*?

Maybe this is why: the next-generation Ducati V-twin
nears completion at Borgo Panigale in August 1986. Standing
behind the prototype water-cooled, dohc, eight-valve desmo
V-twin are Taglioni and his young successor Massimo Bordi,
whose first design this is. Judging by the way it stunned race-
watchers with its speed on its début six weeks later in the
Bol d'Or 24-hour race, then in Lucchinelli's ride to victory at
Daytona the following March (when he clocked 166 mph on
the banking on an 851 cc twin), Bordi has good cause to look
satisfied

The heart of the new engine, seen here at Daytona, is the Weber engine management system which controls ignition and fuel injection by means of a pre-programmable microchip and on-board computer. In adapting this system, used successfully on four wheels for some years, to motorcycles for the first time, Ducati and Weber scored a notable advance in two-wheeled technology

Above

The eight-valve Ducati originally used standard Pantah crankcases, before an all-new, and stronger, bottom end arrived in the spring of 1987

Left

Each compact cylinder head was a masterpiece of design and casting. Bordi consulted Cosworth design chief Keith Duckworth before penning his engine, resulting in an ultra-flat included valve angle of 40 degrees

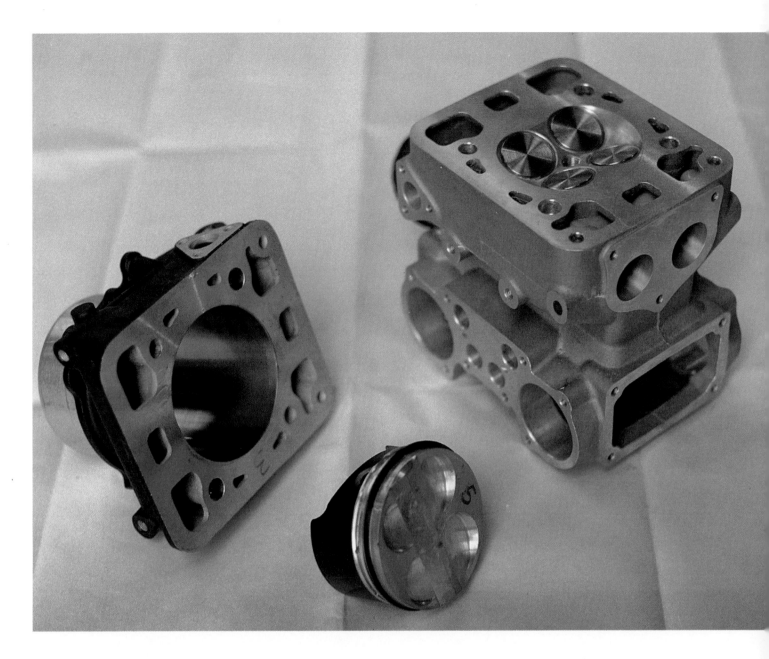

Incredible as it seemed, the factory eight-valver was a desmo;
each cylinder head contained four valves and eight rockers,
but no valve springs

Above and below
Four-lobe camshafts and water-pump with special outer cover are also finely made

Right
Marco Lucchinelli in reflective mood before the start of the 1987 Daytona BoTT race. He needn't have worried; even with a wrongly programmed EMS microchip, his eight-valve 850 desmo was streets faster than the opposition

Another example of Australasian enterprise, Ducatistically-speaking, is Western Australian Brook Henry's big twin, bored to 905 cc and with direct belt drive to the camshafts from the crank substituted for the original bevel-drive system. Unlike the Pantah, the lower belt pulley is fitted directly to the crankshaft, therefore the belts run at engine speed, though without apparent detriment. The forward cambelt cover is plastic. Crankshaft weight has been reduced by 50 per cent by machining. Krober ignition, self-made 60-degree heads and a beefed-up, reworked chassis with alloy swing arm are just some of the features of this remarkable bike, which won the WA Thunderbikes series in 1985 in the hands of rider Brendan Johnson

Above

The 1973 F750 bike featured eccentric adjustment of wheelbase and chain alignment at the swing-arm pivot plus a choice of locations for the rear axle, but would have been fitted with conventional forks rather than the 1972-type leading-axle design used here

Overleaf

Three historic Ducatis, the property of Spanish enthusiast and expert classic racer Joaquin Folch, lined up on the pit straight at Calafat. Left is the 900 which won the 1980 Barcelona 24 Horas ridden by Mallol and Tejedo; centre, one of the factory F750 machines dating from 1973; and on the right, the 750TT1 which won the Barcelona marathon in 1984, ridden by Grau, Garriga and Reyes. All are in perfect restored, ready-to-race, condition

Above

This well-restored bike has a dry clutch and is believed to be the machine ridden by Bruno Kneubuhler in the 1973 Imola 200, the first heat of which he led before falling

Right

The 1973 works engine was a short-stroke 86 × 64.5 mm engine (rather than the previous 80 × 74.4 mm unit), with narrower powerband but capable of higher revs. The desmo engine delivered 89 bhp at 10,000 rpm, but was adjudged less satisfactory then the more flexible, lower revving if less powerful, longer-stroke unit. For Ing. Taglioni, less has sometimes been more

Kneubuhler at speed on the 750 at Imola in 1973. Note the
frame similarities with the Folch bike, but the later-type forks

Above

Jose Maria Mallol (left) and Alejandro Tejedo (second from right) reacquaint themselves with their 1980 Montjuich-winning bike, together with Ducati team manager Ricardo Fargas and (right) mechanic Francisco Castellanos, who rebuilt the engine for present owner Joaquin Folch

Right

The twin fillers have small tabs brazed on to them to prevent them jamming

Above

The lightly modified 860 cc engine has numerous small touches to make it an endurance champion—like this dipstick to permit speedy checks of the oil level at pit stops

Left

The headlamp has a butterfly adjuster to ensure the correct beam level for Montjuich's twisty track at night

Overleaf

Essentially an NCR-modified 900SS built for the FIM's new Silhouette endurance class in 1978, the Montjuich winner must surely be one of the most elegantly purposeful Ducatis ever built

Previous page
This 1984 Montjuich victor is a standard customer 750TT1 racer and was number 24 out of the first batch of 25, built in 1983

Above
A cantilever rear works OK on smooth tracks, but hops and skips on bumpy circuits like Calafat or the Isle of Man

Right
With its acquisition by the Castiglioni brothers' Cagiva concern in 1985, Ducati entered a new and hopefully more prosperous future in which the identity of the 'connoisseur's motorcycle' will be safeguarded. In 1986, Husqvarna joined the family, leading to this cosy ad in Italian magazines. Early in 1987, Morini—another old-established Italian company with a historic past—joined the fold. Who's next?

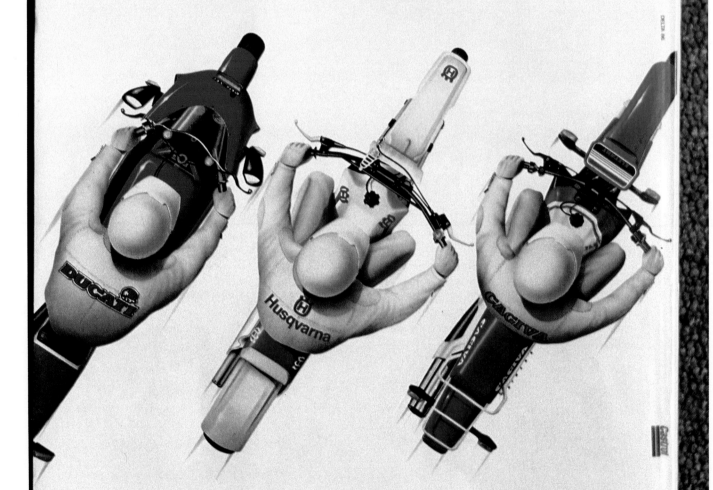

INSIEME SULLE STRADE DEL MONDO

GRUPPO: DUCATI - HUSQVARNA - CAGIVA

Other motorcycle titles from Osprey are listed on the
inside of the back jacket